MW00948302

CHALLENGES AND GROWTH

JOURNAL

A COMPANION WORKBOOK TO BRAIN TRAINING
FOR THE HIGHLY SENSITIVE PERSON

JULIE BJELLAND, LMFT

Designed by Jeanly Fresh M. Zamora

ISBN-13: 978-1-9762-4295-3

DEDICATION

This book is dedicated to all of you who are working to find yourself, love and accept yourself, and live an authentic life being "YOU."

CONTENTS

INTRODUCTION

It is often second nature for highly sensitive persons (HSPs) to focus on what we perceive as our faults instead of focusing on our strengths. We might be hard on ourselves for being "overly sensitive" to the words or actions of another, but it is important to consider that our sensitivity to emotions and situations allows us to be more empathetic than 80 to 85 percent of the population. It is our sensitivities that offer us many other gifts as well. One of the first steps to living our best lives as our true selves is in realizing the unique challenges we, as HSPs, face.

This Challenges and Growth Journal, a companion workbook to *Brain Training for the Highly Sensitive Person,* is designed to help you identify the challenges in your life and focus on specific ways you can overcome these challenges. Profound growth often follows challenge.

Use this companion workbook each week as you learn and practice the brain-training techniques laid out in the book. This workbook is a place for you to record your emotional and sensory triggers, your fears, and the areas that you want to have growth in. As you do this, you will begin to identify which techniques help you prevent your triggers from sending you into the spiral of emotional reaction. At the same time, you will use the Positives Journal companion workbook to record all of your successes, your strengths, and your gifts so that you can truly begin to be the YOU you were meant to be.

WEEK ONE REFLECTIONS

What are the things that you feel affect you as an HSP?

_____

_____

_____

_____

_____

_____

_____

_____

What are the things that you find to be hard or challenging as an HSP?

_____

_____

_____

_____

_____

_____

_____

_____

What are the things you wish you could change?

_____

_____

_____

_____

_____

_____

_____

In your Positives Journal this week, you were asked to speak to a few people you are close to and have them send you a list of what they see as positives about you. If you really struggle with asking people about your positives, in the space below explore why that is so hard for you. You might also suggest to the people you ask that you name their positives too. This can make asking for your positives a little easier.

_____

_____

_____

_____

_____

_____

_____

Additional Thoughts

WEEK TWO REFLECTIONS

What body sensations do you observe about yourself when you are in your limbic system?

_____

_____

_____

_____

_____

_____

_____

_____

As you consciously pay attention to times you activate your limbic system, what patterns do you observe?

_____

_____

_____

_____

_____

_____

_____

_____

Are there certain people, situations, times of day, etc., that you notice create triggers for your limbic system? Describe them here.

_____

_____

_____

_____

_____

_____

_____

Have you observed ways in which you may have perfectionistic expectations of yourself?

_____

_____

_____

_____

_____

_____

_____

Are there ways you can be less hard on yourself?

_____

_____

_____

_____

_____

_____

_____

_____

Sunday

Today, I observed and identified the following body sensations when I may have had an activated limbic system . . .

_____

_____

_____

_____

Today, I observed that the following people or situations felt triggering to me . . .

_____

_____

_____

_____

In the future, I can make these less triggering by . . .

_____

_____

_____

_____

Today, I recognized I was using a perfectionist measurement tool and . . .

_____

_____

_____

Monday

Today, I observed and identified the following body sensations when I may have had an activated limbic system . . .

_____

_____

_____

_____

Today, I observed that the following people or situations felt triggering to me . . .

_____

_____

_____

_____

In the future, I can make these less triggering by . . .

_____

_____

_____

_____

Today, I recognized I was using a perfectionist measurement tool and . . .

_____

_____

_____

Tuesday

Today, I observed and identified the following body sensations when I may have had an activated limbic system . . .

_____

_____

_____

_____

Today, I observed that the following people or situations felt triggering to me . . .

_____

_____

_____

_____

In the future, I can make these less triggering by . . .

_____

_____

_____

_____

Today, I recognized I was using a perfectionist measurement tool and . . .

_____

_____

_____

Wednesday

Today, I observed and identified the following body sensations when I may have had an activated limbic system . . .

_____

_____

_____

_____

Today, I observed that the following people or situations felt triggering to me . . .

_____

_____

_____

_____

In the future, I can make these less triggering by . . .

_____

_____

_____

_____

Today, I recognized I was using a perfectionist measurement tool and . . .

_____

_____

_____

Thursday

Today, I observed and identified the following body sensations when I may have had an activated limbic system . . .

_____

_____

_____

_____

Today, I observed that the following people or situations felt triggering to me . . .

_____

_____

_____

_____

In the future, I can make these less triggering by . . .

_____

_____

_____

_____

Today, I recognized I was using a perfectionist measurement tool and . . .

_____

_____

_____

Friday

Today, I observed and identified the following body sensations when I may have had an activated limbic system . . .

_____

_____

_____

_____

Today, I observed that the following people or situations felt triggering to me . . .

_____

_____

_____

_____

In the future, I can make these less triggering by . . .

_____

_____

_____

_____

Today, I recognized I was using a perfectionist measurement tool and . . .

_____

_____

_____

Saturday

Today, I observed and identified the following body sensations when I may have had an activated limbic system . . .

_____

_____

_____

_____

Today, I observed that the following people or situations felt triggering to me . . .

_____

_____

_____

_____

In the future, I can make these less triggering by . . .

_____

_____

_____

_____

Today, I recognized I was using a perfectionist measurement tool and . . .

_____

_____

_____

Additional Thoughts

WEEK THREE REFLECTIONS

Write down ways in which you observed you were not compassionate with yourself.

_____

_____

_____

_____

_____

_____

_____

_____

What emotions do you label as bad or wrong? Do you notice you add that thousand-pound weight of judgment onto certain emotions?

_____

_____

_____

_____

_____

_____

_____

_____

What things did you say that sounded hard on yourself? Would you say those things to someone you love? How does it feel when you say those things to yourself? How would you like to change this?

_____

_____

_____

_____

_____

_____

_____

Sunday

Today, I observed and identified the following body sensations when I may have had an activated limbic system . . .

_____

_____

Today, I observed that these people or situations felt triggering to me . . .

_____

_____

In the future, I can make these less triggering by . . .

_____

_____

I recognized I was using a perfectionist measurement tool today and . . .

_____

_____

I observed and identified these ways in which I was not compassionate with myself today . . .

_____

_____

If I was being compassionate with myself, I would have said this . . .

_____

_____

Monday

Today, I observed and identified the following body sensations when I may have had an activated limbic system . . .

_____

_____

Today, I observed that these people or situations felt triggering to me . . .

_____

_____

In the future, I can make these less triggering by . . .

_____

_____

I recognized I was using a perfectionist measurement tool today and . . .

_____

_____

I observed and identified these ways in which I was not compassionate with myself today . . .

_____

_____

If I was being compassionate with myself, I would have said this . . .

_____

_____

Tuesday

Today, I observed and identified the following body sensations when I may have had an activated limbic system . . .

_____

_____

Today, I observed that these people or situations felt triggering to me . . .

_____

_____

In the future, I can make these less triggering by . . .

_____

_____

I recognized I was using a perfectionist measurement tool today and . . .

_____

_____

I observed and identified these ways in which I was not compassionate with myself today . . .

_____

_____

If I was being compassionate with myself, I would have said this . . .

_____

_____

Wednesday

Today, I observed and identified the following body sensations when I may have had an activated limbic system . . .

_____

_____

Today, I observed that these people or situations felt triggering to me . . .

_____

_____

In the future, I can make these less triggering by . . .

_____

_____

I recognized I was using a perfectionist measurement tool today and . . .

_____

_____

I observed and identified these ways in which I was not compassionate with myself today . . .

_____

_____

If I was being compassionate with myself, I would have said this . . .

_____

_____

Thursday

Today, I observed and identified the following body sensations when I may have had an activated limbic system . . .

_____

_____

Today, I observed that these people or situations felt triggering to me . . .

_____

_____

In the future, I can make these less triggering by . . .

_____

_____

I recognized I was using a perfectionist measurement tool today and . . .

_____

_____

I observed and identified these ways in which I was not compassionate with myself today . . .

_____

_____

If I was being compassionate with myself, I would have said this . . .

_____

_____

Friday

Today, I observed and identified the following body sensations when I may have had an activated limbic system . . .

_____

_____

Today, I observed that these people or situations felt triggering to me . . .

_____

_____

In the future, I can make these less triggering by . . .

_____

_____

I recognized I was using a perfectionist measurement tool today and . . .

_____

_____

I observed and identified these ways in which I was not compassionate with myself today . . .

_____

_____

If I was being compassionate with myself, I would have said this . . .

_____

_____

Saturday

Today, I observed and identified the following body sensations when I may have had an activated limbic system . . .

_____

_____

Today, I observed that these people or situations felt triggering to me . . .

_____

_____

In the future, I can make these less triggering by . . .

_____

_____

I recognized I was using a perfectionist measurement tool today and . . .

_____

_____

I observed and identified these ways in which I was not compassionate with myself today . . .

_____

_____

If I was being compassionate with myself, I would have said this . . .

_____

_____

Additional Thoughts

WEEK FOUR REFLECTIONS

What situations arose that activated your limbic system this week?

_____

_____

_____

_____

_____

What did you observe physically and emotionally when you felt activated?

_____

_____

_____

_____

_____

_____

Were you too hard on yourself at any time this week?

_____

_____

_____

_____

_____

_____

_____

_____

If this happens again, how can you show compassion toward yourself?

_____

_____

_____

_____

_____

_____

_____

Practice checking in with yourself. Ask yourself:

How am I doing?

_____

_____

_____

Is there anything bothering me right now?

_____

_____

_____

What is my stress number?

_____

_____

_____

Do I need to do anything to feel better right now?

_____

_____

_____

Is there anything I need to do to improve my sleep? What will I try to do to improve it?

_____

_____

_____

_____

Sunday

Today, I observed and identified these body sensations when I may have had an activated limbic system . . .

_____

_____

Today, I observed that these people or situations felt triggering to me . . .

_____

_____

In the future, I can make these less triggering by . . .

_____

_____

I recognized I was using a perfectionist measurement tool today and . . .

_____

_____

I observed and identified these ways in which I was not compassionate with myself today . . .

_____

_____

If I was being compassionate with myself, I would have said this . . .

_____

_____

Today, my stress number reached ___. I worked to lower that number by . . .

_____

_____

Monday

Today, I observed and identified these body sensations when I may have had an activated limbic system . . .

_____

_____

Today, I observed that these people or situations felt triggering to me . . .

_____

_____

In the future, I can make these less triggering by . . .

_____

_____

I recognized I was using a perfectionist measurement tool today and . . .

_____

_____

I observed and identified these ways in which I was not compassionate with myself today . . .

_____

_____

If I was being compassionate with myself, I would have said this . . .

_____

_____

Today, my stress number reached ____. I worked to lower that number by . . .

_____

_____

Tuesday

Today, I observed and identified these body sensations when I may have had an activated limbic system . . .

_____

_____

Today, I observed that these people or situations felt triggering to me . . .

_____

_____

In the future, I can make these less triggering by . . .

_____

_____

I recognized I was using a perfectionist measurement tool today and . . .

_____

_____

I observed and identified these ways in which I was not compassionate with myself today . . .

_____

_____

If I was being compassionate with myself, I would have said this . . .

_____

_____

Today, my stress number reached ____. I worked to lower that number by . . .

_____

_____

Wednesday

Today, I observed and identified these body sensations when I may have had an activated limbic system . . .

_____

_____

Today, I observed that these people or situations felt triggering to me . . .

_____

_____

In the future, I can make these less triggering by . . .

_____

_____

I recognized I was using a perfectionist measurement tool today and . . .

_____

_____

I observed and identified these ways in which I was not compassionate with myself today . . .

_____

_____

If I was being compassionate with myself, I would have said this . . .

_____

_____

Today, my stress number reached ___. I worked to lower that number by . . .

_____

_____

Thursday

Today, I observed and identified these body sensations when I may have had an activated limbic system . . .

_____

_____

Today, I observed that these people or situations felt triggering to me . . .

_____

_____

In the future, I can make these less triggering by . . .

_____

_____

I recognized I was using a perfectionist measurement tool today and . . .

_____

_____

I observed and identified these ways in which I was not compassionate with myself today . . .

_____

_____

If I was being compassionate with myself, I would have said this . . .

_____

_____

Today, my stress number reached ___. I worked to lower that number by . . .

_____

_____

Friday

Today, I observed and identified these body sensations when I may have had an activated limbic system . . .

_____

_____

Today, I observed that these people or situations felt triggering to me . . .

_____

_____

In the future, I can make these less triggering by . . .

_____

_____

I recognized I was using a perfectionist measurement tool today and . . .

_____

_____

I observed and identified these ways in which I was not compassionate with myself today . . .

_____

_____

If I was being compassionate with myself, I would have said this . . .

_____

_____

Today, my stress number reached ___. I worked to lower that number by . . .

_____

_____

Saturday

Today, I observed and identified these body sensations when I may have had an activated limbic system . . .

_____

_____

Today, I observed that these people or situations felt triggering to me . . .

_____

_____

In the future, I can make these less triggering by . . .

_____

_____

I recognized I was using a perfectionist measurement tool today and . . .

_____

_____

I observed and identified these ways in which I was not compassionate with myself today . . .

_____

_____

If I was being compassionate with myself, I would have said this . . .

_____

_____

Today, my stress number reached ____. I worked to lower that number by . . .

_____

_____

Additional Thoughts

WEEK FIVE REFLECTIONS

What perfectionist tendencies did I identify this week?

_____

_____

_____

_____

_____

_____

_____

What emotional, irrational-brain messages did I observe? What cognitive, rational facts did I use to counter them?

_____

_____

_____

_____

_____

_____

_____

_____

Can I identify some of my main core emotional messages? What are they?

_____

_____

_____

_____

_____

_____

_____

Describe a trigger you experienced this week and the tools you used to counteract the trigger.

_____

_____

_____

_____

_____

_____

_____

Sunday

Today, I observed and identified these body sensations when I may have had an activated limbic system . . .

_____

_____

Today, I observed that these people, situations, or emotions felt triggering to me . . .

_____

_____

In the future, I can make these less triggering by . . .

_____

_____

I recognized I was using a perfectionist measurement tool today and . . .

_____

_____

I observed and identified these ways in which I was not compassionate with myself today . . .

_____

_____

If I was being compassionate with myself, I would have said this . . .

_____

_____

Today, my stress number reached ____. I worked to lower that number by . . .

_____

_____

Monday

Today, I observed and identified these body sensations when I may have had an activated limbic system . . .

_____

_____

Today, I observed that these people, situations, or emotions felt triggering to me . . .

_____

_____

In the future, I can make these less triggering by . . .

_____

_____

I recognized I was using a perfectionist measurement tool today and . . .

_____

_____

I observed and identified these ways in which I was not compassionate with myself today . . .

_____

_____

If I was being compassionate with myself, I would have said this . . .

_____

_____

Today, my stress number reached ____. I worked to lower that number by . . .

_____

_____

Tuesday

Today, I observed and identified these body sensations when I may have had an activated limbic system . . .

_____

_____

Today, I observed that these people, situations, or emotions felt triggering to me . . .

_____

_____

In the future, I can make these less triggering by . . .

_____

_____

I recognized I was using a perfectionist measurement tool today and . . .

_____

_____

I observed and identified these ways in which I was not compassionate with myself today . . .

_____

_____

If I was being compassionate with myself, I would have said this . . .

_____

_____

Today, my stress number reached ___. I worked to lower that number by . . .

_____

_____

Wednesday

Today, I observed and identified these body sensations when I may have had an activated limbic system . . .

_____

_____

Today, I observed that these people, situations, or emotions felt triggering to me . . .

_____

_____

In the future, I can make these less triggering by . . .

_____

_____

I recognized I was using a perfectionist measurement tool today and . . .

_____

_____

I observed and identified these ways in which I was not compassionate with myself today . . .

_____

_____

If I was being compassionate with myself, I would have said this . . .

_____

_____

Today, my stress number reached ____. I worked to lower that number by . . .

_____

_____

Thursday

Today, I observed and identified these body sensations when I may have had an activated limbic system . . .

_____

_____

Today, I observed that these people, situations, or emotions felt triggering to me . . .

_____

_____

In the future, I can make these less triggering by . . .

_____

_____

I recognized I was using a perfectionist measurement tool today and . . .

_____

_____

I observed and identified these ways in which I was not compassionate with myself today . . .

_____

_____

If I was being compassionate with myself, I would have said this . . .

_____

_____

Today, my stress number reached ____. I worked to lower that number by . . .

_____

_____

Friday

Today, I observed and identified these body sensations when I may have had an activated limbic system . . .

_____

_____

Today, I observed that these people, situations, or emotions felt triggering to me . . .

_____

_____

In the future, I can make these less triggering by . . .

_____

_____

I recognized I was using a perfectionist measurement tool today and . . .

_____

_____

I observed and identified these ways in which I was not compassionate with myself today . . .

_____

_____

If I was being compassionate with myself, I would have said this . . .

_____

_____

Today, my stress number reached ____. I worked to lower that number by . . .

_____

_____

Saturday

Today, I observed and identified these body sensations when I may have had an activated limbic system . . .

_____

_____

Today, I observed that these people, situations, or emotions felt triggering to me . . .

_____

_____

In the future, I can make these less triggering by . . .

_____

_____

I recognized I was using a perfectionist measurement tool today and . . .

_____

_____

I observed and identified these ways in which I was not compassionate with myself today . . .

_____

_____

If I was being compassionate with myself, I would have said this . . .

_____

_____

Today, my stress number reached ____. I worked to lower that number by . . .

_____

_____

Additional Thoughts

Explore all the areas of potential sensory triggers in your life and record them here.

_____

_____

_____

_____

_____

_____

_____

_____

When do you observe your stress levels or anxiety levels increase?

_____

_____

_____

_____

_____

_____

_____

After you notice you have been triggered, what kinds of feelings or emotions do you experience?

_____

_____

_____

_____

_____

_____

_____

How do you know you are triggered? What physical or emotional symptoms do you experience when you have experienced sensory triggers?

_____

_____

_____

_____

_____

_____

_____

What do you observe to be some of your biggest energy zappers?

_____

_____

_____

_____

_____

_____

_____

If you hear yourself saying that you should or shouldn't do something, take a look at that and ask yourself what your needs are. What have you observed about why you think you "should" or "shouldn't" do or feel something? Can you make changes here?

_____

_____

_____

_____

_____

_____

_____

What kinds of changes can you make in your home and/or work environments to reduce sensory triggers?

_____

_____

_____

_____

_____

_____

_____

Sunday

Today, I observed and identified these body sensations when I may have had an activated limbic system . . .

_____

Today, I observed that these people, situations, or emotions felt triggering to me . . .

_____

In the future, I can make these less triggering by . . .

_____

I recognized I was using a perfectionist measurement tool today and . . .

_____

I observed and identified these ways in which I was not compassionate with myself today . . .

_____

If I was being compassionate with myself, I would have said this . . .

_____

Today, my stress number reached ____. I worked to lower that number by . . .

_____

Today, I observed and identified these sensory triggers . . .

_____

I might be able to reduce these sensory triggers in the future by . . .

_____

Monday

Today, I observed and identified these body sensations when I may have had an activated limbic system . . .

Today, I observed that these people, situations, or emotions felt triggering to me . . .

In the future, I can make these less triggering by . . .

I recognized I was using a perfectionist measurement tool today and . . .

I observed and identified these ways in which I was not compassionate with myself today . . .

If I was being compassionate with myself, I would have said this . . .

Today, my stress number reached ____. I worked to lower that number by . . .

Today, I observed and identified these sensory triggers . . .

I might be able to reduce these sensory triggers in the future by . . .

Tuesday

Today, I observed and identified these body sensations when I may have had an activated limbic system . . .

_____

Today, I observed that these people, situations, or emotions felt triggering to me . . .

_____

In the future, I can make these less triggering by . . .

_____

I recognized I was using a perfectionist measurement tool today and . . .

_____

I observed and identified these ways in which I was not compassionate with myself today . . .

_____

If I was being compassionate with myself, I would have said this . . .

_____

Today, my stress number reached ____. I worked to lower that number by . . .

_____

Today, I observed and identified these sensory triggers . . .

_____

I might be able to reduce these sensory triggers in the future by . . .

_____

Wednesday

Today, I observed and identified these body sensations when I may have had an activated limbic system . . .

_____

Today, I observed that these people, situations, or emotions felt triggering to me . . .

_____

In the future, I can make these less triggering by . . .

_____

I recognized I was using a perfectionist measurement tool today and . . .

_____

I observed and identified these ways in which I was not compassionate with myself today . . .

_____

If I was being compassionate with myself, I would have said this . . .

_____

Today, my stress number reached ____. I worked to lower that number by . . .

_____

Today, I observed and identified these sensory triggers . . .

_____

I might be able to reduce these sensory triggers in the future by . . .

_____

Thursday

Today, I observed and identified these body sensations when I may have had an activated limbic system . . .

_____

Today, I observed that these people, situations, or emotions felt triggering to me . . .

_____

In the future, I can make these less triggering by . . .

_____

I recognized I was using a perfectionist measurement tool today and . . .

_____

I observed and identified these ways in which I was not compassionate with myself today . . .

_____

If I was being compassionate with myself, I would have said this . . .

_____

Today, my stress number reached ___. I worked to lower that number by . . .

_____

Today, I observed and identified these sensory triggers . . .

_____

I might be able to reduce these sensory triggers in the future by . . .

_____

Friday

Today, I observed and identified these body sensations when I may have had an activated limbic system . . .

_____

Today, I observed that these people, situations, or emotions felt triggering to me . . .

_____

In the future, I can make these less triggering by . . .

_____

I recognized I was using a perfectionist measurement tool today and . . .

_____

I observed and identified these ways in which I was not compassionate with myself today . . .

_____

If I was being compassionate with myself, I would have said this . . .

_____

Today, my stress number reached ____. I worked to lower that number by . . .

_____

Today, I observed and identified these sensory triggers . . .

_____

I might be able to reduce these sensory triggers in the future by . . .

_____

Saturday

Today, I observed and identified these body sensations when I may have had an activated limbic system . . .

_____

Today, I observed that these people, situations, or emotions felt triggering to me . . .

_____

In the future, I can make these less triggering by . . .

_____

I recognized I was using a perfectionist measurement tool today and . . .

_____

I observed and identified these ways in which I was not compassionate with myself today . . .

_____

If I was being compassionate with myself, I would have said this . . .

_____

Today, my stress number reached ____. I worked to lower that number by . . .

_____

Today, I observed and identified these sensory triggers . . .

_____

I might be able to reduce these sensory triggers in the future by . . .

_____

Additional Thoughts

What situations arose that activated your limbic system this week?

_____

_____

_____

_____

_____

_____

_____

How did you handle the situation?

_____

_____

_____

_____

_____

_____

_____

_____

Were you too hard on yourself at any time this week?

_____

_____

_____

_____

_____

_____

_____

If this happens again, how can you show compassion toward yourself?

_____

_____

_____

_____

_____

_____

_____

Have you been able to reduce the storm of emotional reactions, triggers, and overstimulation? In what ways?

_____

_____

_____

_____

_____

_____

_____

Sunday

Today, I observed and identified these body sensations when I may have had an activated limbic system . . .

_____

Today, I observed that these people, situations, or emotions felt triggering to me . . .

_____

In the future, I can make these less triggering by . . .

_____

I recognized I was using a perfectionist measurement tool today and . . .

_____

I observed and identified these ways in which I was not compassionate with myself today . . .

_____

If I was being compassionate with myself, I would have said this . . .

_____

Today, my stress number reached ____. I worked to lower that number by . . .

_____

Today, I observed and identified these sensory triggers . . .

_____

I might be able to reduce these sensory triggers in the future by . . .

_____

Monday

Today, I observed and identified these body sensations when I may have had an activated limbic system . . .

_____

Today, I observed that these people, situations, or emotions felt triggering to me . . .

_____

In the future, I can make these less triggering by . . .

_____

I recognized I was using a perfectionist measurement tool today and . . .

_____

I observed and identified these ways in which I was not compassionate with myself today . . .

_____

If I was being compassionate with myself, I would have said this . . .

_____

Today, my stress number reached ____. I worked to lower that number by . . .

_____

Today, I observed and identified these sensory triggers . . .

_____

I might be able to reduce these sensory triggers in the future by . . .

_____

Tuesday

Today, I observed and identified these body sensations when I may have had an activated limbic system . . .

Today, I observed that these people, situations, or emotions felt triggering to me . . .

In the future, I can make these less triggering by . . .

I recognized I was using a perfectionist measurement tool today and . . .

I observed and identified these ways in which I was not compassionate with myself today . . .

If I was being compassionate with myself, I would have said this . . .

Today, my stress number reached ___. I worked to lower that number by . . .

Today, I observed and identified these sensory triggers . . .

I might be able to reduce these sensory triggers in the future by . . .

Wednesday

Today, I observed and identified these body sensations when I may have had an activated limbic system . . .

_____

Today, I observed that these people, situations, or emotions felt triggering to me . . .

_____

In the future, I can make these less triggering by . . .

_____

I recognized I was using a perfectionist measurement tool today and . . .

_____

I observed and identified these ways in which I was not compassionate with myself today . . .

_____

If I was being compassionate with myself, I would have said this . . .

_____

Today, my stress number reached ____. I worked to lower that number by . . .

_____

Today, I observed and identified these sensory triggers . . .

_____

I might be able to reduce these sensory triggers in the future by . . .

_____

Thursday

Today, I observed and identified these body sensations when I may have had an activated limbic system . . .

_____

Today, I observed that these people, situations, or emotions felt triggering to me . . .

_____

In the future, I can make these less triggering by . . .

_____

I recognized I was using a perfectionist measurement tool today and . . .

_____

I observed and identified these ways in which I was not compassionate with myself today . . .

_____

If I was being compassionate with myself, I would have said this . . .

_____

Today, my stress number reached ____. I worked to lower that number by . . .

_____

Today, I observed and identified these sensory triggers . . .

_____

I might be able to reduce these sensory triggers in the future by . . .

_____

Friday

Today, I observed and identified these body sensations when I may have had an activated limbic system . . .

Today, I observed that these people, situations, or emotions felt triggering to me . . .

In the future, I can make these less triggering by . . .

I recognized I was using a perfectionist measurement tool today and . . .

I observed and identified these ways in which I was not compassionate with myself today . . .

If I was being compassionate with myself, I would have said this . . .

Today, my stress number reached ____. I worked to lower that number by . . .

Today, I observed and identified these sensory triggers . . .

I might be able to reduce these sensory triggers in the future by . . .

Saturday

Today, I observed and identified these body sensations when I may have had an activated limbic system . . .

_____

Today, I observed that these people, situations, or emotions felt triggering to me . . .

_____

In the future, I can make these less triggering by . . .

_____

I recognized I was using a perfectionist measurement tool today and . . .

_____

I observed and identified these ways in which I was not compassionate with myself today . . .

_____

If I was being compassionate with myself, I would have said this . . .

_____

Today, my stress number reached ____. I worked to lower that number by . . .

_____

Today, I observed and identified these sensory triggers . . .

_____

I might be able to reduce these sensory triggers in the future by . . .

_____

Additional Thoughts

WEEK EIGHT REFLECTIONS

We learned a lot about our trait and how we can begin to re-label and reframe our past experiences and thoughts about ourselves. Have you been able to re-label things about yourself?

_____

_____

_____

_____

_____

_____

_____

What have you learned about your emotional limbic system brain?

_____

_____

_____

_____

_____

_____

_____

What have you observed are things you can do to help you stay centered and grounded so you don't trigger the limbic system?

_____

_____

_____

_____

_____

_____

_____

Have you been able to be consistent with self-compassion and nurturing? If not, what is getting in your way?

_____

_____

_____

_____

_____

_____

_____

Reflect on where you were when you started this book and where you are now. Have you met some of your goals?

_____

_____

_____

_____

_____

_____

_____

What specific activities and/or experiences have you been choosing to reduce your stress numbers?

_____

_____

_____

_____

_____

_____

_____

Are there things that used to trigger you that you have observed trigger you less now?

_____

_____

_____

_____

_____

_____

_____

_____

Do you notice that you have that "pause-and-check" space right before the route to the limbic system?

_____

_____

_____

_____

_____

_____

_____

_____

What were you able to identify as some of your main sensory triggers?

_____

_____

_____

_____

_____

_____

_____

In what ways have you been able to reduce the sensory overload?

_____

_____

_____

_____

_____

_____

_____

Have you been able to increase more of your unstructured alone time? In what ways?

_____

_____

_____

_____

_____

_____

_____

Have you found ways to reduce your guilt, shame, blame, and resentment? What factors help you reduce these?

_____

_____

_____

_____

_____

_____

_____

Can you now prioritize yourself more? Name some examples.

_____

_____

_____

_____

_____

_____

_____

What types of commitment to yourself are you going to make from now on to help you feel better and live your best life?

_____

_____

_____

_____

_____

_____

_____

In what ways do you still want to grow? What would you need in order to grow in these areas?

_____

_____

_____

_____

_____

_____

_____

Reflect on what this journey has meant to you.

_____

_____

_____

_____

_____

_____

_____

Sunday

Today, I observed and identified these body sensations when I may have had an activated limbic system . . .

_____

Today, I observed that these people, situations, or emotions felt triggering to me . . .

_____

In the future, I can make these less triggering by . . .

_____

I recognized I was using a perfectionist measurement tool today and . . .

_____

I observed and identified these ways in which I was not compassionate with myself today . . .

_____

If I was being compassionate with myself, I would have said this . . .

_____

Today, my stress number reached ____. I worked to lower that number by . . .

_____

Today, I observed and identified these sensory triggers . . .

_____

I might be able to reduce these sensory triggers in the future by . . .

_____

Monday

Today, I observed and identified these body sensations when I may have had an activated limbic system . . .

_____

Today, I observed that these people, situations, or emotions felt triggering to me . . .

_____

In the future, I can make these less triggering by . . .

_____

I recognized I was using a perfectionist measurement tool today and . . .

_____

I observed and identified these ways in which I was not compassionate with myself today . . .

_____

If I was being compassionate with myself, I would have said this . . .

_____

Today, my stress number reached ____. I worked to lower that number by . . .

_____

Today, I observed and identified these sensory triggers . . .

_____

I might be able to reduce these sensory triggers in the future by . . .

_____

Tuesday

Today, I observed and identified these body sensations when I may have had an activated limbic system . . .

_____

Today, I observed that these people, situations, or emotions felt triggering to me . . .

_____

In the future, I can make these less triggering by . . .

_____

I recognized I was using a perfectionist measurement tool today and . . .

_____

I observed and identified these ways in which I was not compassionate with myself today . . .

_____

If I was being compassionate with myself, I would have said this . . .

_____

Today, my stress number reached ____. I worked to lower that number by . . .

_____

Today, I observed and identified these sensory triggers . . .

_____

I might be able to reduce these sensory triggers in the future by . . .

_____

Wednesday

Today, I observed and identified these body sensations when I may have had an activated limbic system . . .

_____

Today, I observed that these people, situations, or emotions felt triggering to me . . .

_____

In the future, I can make these less triggering by . . .

_____

I recognized I was using a perfectionist measurement tool today and . . .

_____

I observed and identified these ways in which I was not compassionate with myself today . . .

_____

If I was being compassionate with myself, I would have said this . . .

_____

Today, my stress number reached ____. I worked to lower that number by . . .

_____

Today, I observed and identified these sensory triggers . . .

_____

I might be able to reduce these sensory triggers in the future by . . .

_____

Thursday

Today, I observed and identified these body sensations when I may have had an activated limbic system . . .

_____

Today, I observed that these people, situations, or emotions felt triggering to me . . .

_____

In the future, I can make these less triggering by . . .

_____

I recognized I was using a perfectionist measurement tool today and . . .

_____

I observed and identified these ways in which I was not compassionate with myself today . . .

_____

If I was being compassionate with myself, I would have said this . . .

_____

Today, my stress number reached ___. I worked to lower that number by . . .

_____

Today, I observed and identified these sensory triggers . . .

_____

I might be able to reduce these sensory triggers in the future by . . .

_____

Friday

Today, I observed and identified these body sensations when I may have had an activated limbic system . . .

_____

Today, I observed that these people, situations, or emotions felt triggering to me . . .

_____

In the future, I can make these less triggering by . . .

_____

I recognized I was using a perfectionist measurement tool today and . . .

_____

I observed and identified these ways in which I was not compassionate with myself today . . .

_____

If I was being compassionate with myself, I would have said this . . .

_____

Today, my stress number reached ___. I worked to lower that number by . . .

_____

Today, I observed and identified these sensory triggers . . .

_____

I might be able to reduce these sensory triggers in the future by . . .

_____

Saturday

Today, I observed and identified these body sensations when I may have had an activated limbic system . . .

_____

Today, I observed that these people, situations, or emotions felt triggering to me . . .

_____

In the future, I can make these less triggering by . . .

_____

I recognized I was using a perfectionist measurement tool today and . . .

_____

I observed and identified these ways in which I was not compassionate with myself today . . .

_____

If I was being compassionate with myself, I would have said this . . .

_____

Today, my stress number reached ___. I worked to lower that number by . . .

_____

Today, I observed and identified these sensory triggers . . .

_____

I might be able to reduce these sensory triggers in the future by . . .

_____

Additional Thoughts

Congratulations!

You have now completed the journals for the HSP brain-training program. Take some time, celebrate, and be proud of the work you have put into this. If you still have areas you want to work on contact me through my website: www.juliebjelland.com. Our journey is never "done," and we are all continually working on ourselves, but I hope you have found that having this companion book has helped you become a more "trained" HSP and that you have met some of your goals and are noticing that you are starting to live better as an HSP. Since we need to continually grow and train ourselves as HSPs, I encourage you to return to your journals to remember and reflect on how you've grown, and you can continue using the additional pages to record your thoughts.

Take really good care of your beautiful HSP self.

All the best,

Julie

Additional Thoughts

ABOUT THE AUTHOR

Julie is a licensed psychotherapist in California. Having built a successful private practice, Julie continues to expand her reach by developing online brain-training courses, serving as a consultant to other therapists, teaching workshops, and coaching HSPs globally. Her passion and expertise is in neuroscience and determining how to successfully train the brain so people can live their best lives. Her most recent book, *Brain Training for the Highly Sensitive Person: Techniques to Reduce Anxiety and Overwhelming Emotions*, has received outstanding reviews from world-renowned psychologists Tara Brach, PhD, Rick Hanson, PhD, and Ted Zeff, PhD. Julie specializes in working with anxiety and the highly sensitive person (HSP), couple's communication, self-esteem, and the LGBTQQ community. In addition to her work in psychology, she is a former Guide Dogs for the Blind trainer and author of the book *Imagine Life With A Well-Behaved Dog*.

Julie offers many resources for HSPs through her website: www.juliebjelland.com/.

Stay connected to Julie's HSP work and research through her HSP Facebook group: www.facebook.com/HSP.The.Highly.Sensitive.Person/

Made in the USA
Middletown, DE
12 October 2018